What's in this book

This book belongs to

_____

中国的城市 Cities in China

学习内容 Contents

沟通 Communication

认识中国的主要城市
Learn about the main cities in China

生词 New words

★	想	to want
★	北京	Beijing
★	上海	Shanghai
★	楼	building
★	房子	house
★	地方	place
★	哪儿	where
	城市	city
	长城	Great Wall
	香港	Hong Kong
	像	to be like

句式 Sentence patterns

你想来中国吗？

Do you want to come to China?

你想去哪儿呢？

Where do you want to go?

跨学科学习 Project

不同国家的首都

The capital cities of different countries

文化 Cultures

世界奇观——长城

The Great Wall—one of the Wonders of the World

Get ready

1 Have you been to China?

2 What are your impressions of the cities in China?

3 Which city do you want to go in China?

chéng shì
城市

xiǎng
想

你想来中国吗？你知道中国有哪些城市吗？

北京是中国的首都。长城和天安门很有名。

lóu
楼

fáng zi
房子

上海有高高的楼，也有很多漂亮的老房子。

dì fāng

地方

香港不大，但是有很多好玩的地方。

像 xiàng

有人觉得香港和上海很像。你觉
得呢？

nǐ xiǎng qù nǎr ne

你想去哪儿呢？

中国还有很多有意思的城市。你想
去哪儿呢？

9

Let's think

1 Match the tourist attractions to the correct cities.

Beijing

Shanghai

Hong Kong

2 Which city do you want to visit? Draw and talk about it with your friend.

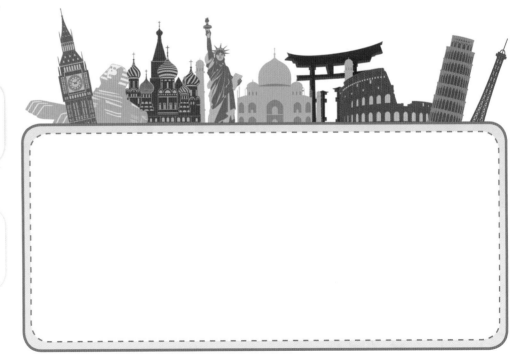

我想去……
因为……

我也喜欢那里，
但是……

New words

02 **1** Learn the new words.

北京

长城

房子

香港

城市

地方

上海

楼

像

哪儿

想

2 Listen to your teacher and point to
the correct words above.

听听说说 Listen and say

 1 Listen and circle the correct answers.

1 女孩想去哪儿?

a 长城

b 香港

c 上海

2 男孩想去香港,为什么?

a 因为那里很好看。

b 因为香港和上海很像。

c 因为香港有很多好玩的地方。

3 男孩在哪儿上课?

a 红色的楼

b 红色的房子

c 高高的楼

2 Look at the pictures. Listen to the story c

 你和浩浩去上美术课吗?

 是,我们最喜欢美术课。

 我想画长城。长城很高、很长……

.

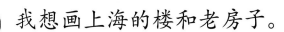 你想画什么？

我想画上海的楼和老房子。

你画的长城真像我画的老房子。

北京

☐ 她想去北京。

☐ 她去想北京。

上海

☐ 上海有高高的楼，也有很多老房子。

☐ 上海有高高的楼，有很多老房子也。

Task

What is the difference between your hometown and China? Paste your photos and say in Chinese.

我的城市有很多好吃的东西，有……

中国有很多好吃的东西。

Paste your photo here.

中国的楼和房子很……

Paste your photo here.

我的城市的楼和房子很……

Game

Compare the two pictures. Circle the nine differences in the picture on the right.

这个地方不一样。这里的树少了……

Chant

 Listen and say.

中国有很多城市，
你知道这几个吗？
首都北京很古老，
有长城和天安门。
上海真是国际化，
人多车多楼也多。
还有香港这地方，
大家都很喜欢它。

生活用语 Daily expressions

太像了！
So similar!

真没想到。
I never knew that.

1 Trace and write the characters.

一 十 才 才 相 相 相 相

相 相 想 想 想

想	想	想	想

一 十 土 圸 圸 地

丶 亠 方 方

地	方	地	方

2 Write and say.

我 ___ 去上海玩。

我想去这个 _____。

3 Read, circle the wrong words and write the correct ones. There is one mistake in each line.

昨天我们一起丢北京了。　　1　_____

北京有很多好玩的地房，我　2　_____

最喜欢长城。我们也相去　　3　_____

上海，去看那里高高的楼扣　4　_____

老房子。

拼音输入法 Pinyin input

1　Look at the characters and the typing methods. Say the words.

kuai			
1 快	2 哭艾	3 苦艾	⬍

ku'ai			
1 酷爱	2 哭艾	3 苦艾	⬍

Some Pinyin syllables have the same letter combination, but they represent one or more characters. We can add the mark (') to break the syllable when the second one starts with 'a', 'e' or 'o'.

2　Add the mark (') to the Pinyin to avoid confusion and write the answers in the boxes. Type the words.

天安门
tiananmen

西安
xian

Cultures

1 Do you know one of the Wonders of the World is in China? Learn about the Great Wall.

长城

The Great Wall of China is a series of fortresses built across the historical northern borders of China.

It was used to protect the states from the invasions.

The Great Wall with all of its branches measures about 21,196 km.

2 Imagine you are on the Great Wall. Draw yourself in the picture and answer the questions.

长城怎么样？那儿好玩吗？你累不累？

长城很……

Project

1 Match the capital cities to the countries. Say the names of the cities in Chinese after your teacher.

> a Washington, D.C.　　b Canberra　　c Cairo
> d New Delhi　　　　　e London　　　f Beijing

中国

英国

美国

India

Egypt

Australia

2 Plan a visit to one of the above cities. Fill in the blanks and talk about the city with your friend.

✈ Boarding Pass

👤 名字：＿＿＿＿＿＿＿＿

✈ 北京—＿＿＿＿＿＿＿＿

📅 ＿＿月＿＿日

✅ ＿＿门　🧳 ＿＿号

……月……日，我想去……因为那个城市很好玩。那儿的楼和房子也很好看，有新的和旧的……

温习 Checkpoint

1. Answer the questions in Chinese and fill in the sentences. Count the points you can get.

中国的城市

+2 a 这是哪个城市？

+2 b 新房子和旧房子像吗？

+3 c 这些楼在哪个城市？

+3 d 这是香港还是上海？

+4 e 这个地方在哪个国家？

+4 f 他们几点去上海？

+5 g 这两个 ☐ ☐ 在哪儿？

+5 h 他们 ☐ 去哪儿？

My points:

☐

2 Work with your friend. Colour the stars and the chillies.

Words	说	读	写
想	☆	☆	☆
北京	☆	☆	🌶
上海	☆	☆	🌶
楼	☆	☆	🌶
房子	☆	☆	🌶
地方	☆	☆	☆
哪儿	☆	☆	🌶
城市	☆	🌶	🌶

Words and sentences	说	读	写
长城	☆	🌶	🌶
香港	☆	🌶	🌶
像	☆	🌶	🌶
你想来中国吗?	☆	☆	🌶
你想去哪儿呢?	☆	☆	🌶

Learn about the main cities in China	☆

3 What does your teacher say?

My teacher says ...

分享 Sharing

Words I remember

想	xiǎng	to want
北京	běi jīng	Beijing
上海	shàng hǎi	Shanghai
楼	lóu	building
房子	fáng zi	house
地方	dì fāng	place
哪儿	nǎr	where
城市	chéng shì	city
长城	cháng chéng	Great Wall
香港	xiāng gǎng	Hong Kong
像	xiàng	to be like

Other words

哪些	nǎ xiē	which
首都	shǒu dū	capital
天安门	tiān ān mén	Tian'anmen
有名	yǒu míng	famous
漂亮	piào liang	beautiful
好玩	hǎo wán	fun
有人	yǒu rén	someone
觉得	jué de	to think
有意思	yǒu yì si	interesting
东西	dōng xi	thing
酷爱	kù ài	to love
西安	xī ān	Xi'an

OXFORD
UNIVERSITY PRESS

Oxford University Press is a department of the University of Oxford.
It furthers the University's objective of excellence in research, scholarship,
and education by publishing worldwide. Oxford is a registered trade mark of
Oxford University Press in the UK and in certain other countries

Published in Hong Kong by
Oxford University Press (China) Limited
39th Floor, One Kowloon, 1 Wang Yuen Street, Kowloon Bay,
Hong Kong

First Edition published in 2017

Illustrated by Anne Lee and Wildman

Photographs for reproduction permitted by Dreamstime.com

China National Publications Import & Export (Group) Corporation is an authorized distributor of
Oxford Elementary Chinese.

Please contact content@cnpiec.com.cn or 86-10-65856782

ISBN: 978-0-19-082255-2

10 9 8 7 6 5 4 3 2